The Perfect Brokerage For You

The Perfect Brokerage For You

The First Step to Create Your

Ultimate Lifestyle as a Real Estate Agent

Randy Zimnoch

The Perfect Brokerage For You:
The First Step to Create Your
Ultimate Lifestyle as a Real Estate Agent
Randy Zimnoch

Published in 2017 by
Randy Zimnoch
San Diego, CA
www.AgentLifestyle.com

Dedication

This book is dedicated to real estate professionals that are making a positive impact in the lives of those they serve, giving generously to others in need, and caring greatly for the ones they love.

This is the ultimate agent lifestyle.

Appreciation

My success in life is not just mine, but the success of a team of powerful contributors…

To my amazing wife and partner, Alycia. Thank you for pushing me to finish this book and helping me so much along the way. #TeamBadase

To my parents who have sacrificed so much as they migrated our family from Poland to America in 1989, giving me endless opportunities in this incredible country. I will never take that for granted.

To my accountability group, Jeff The Machine, Benny The Catalyst and Joey The Zen Master, who have been my personal advising board over the last five years. You guys rock!

Explore, Discover, Evolve!

To Jon Steingraber, my original real estate partner, who encouraged me to take the necessary risks that promoted our success.

To my business partners, Than, Paul, Konrad, and JD for creating an environment of growth-oriented and success-minded individuals and for welcoming me to be a part of it.

To Bryan, the manager at my brokerage for your constant support, incredible commitment and unwavering loyalty. Realty National wouldn't be the same without you.

And lastly, to Nick and Megan from Life on Fire for helping me see the possibilities within what I've created, for leading me to meet my wife and introducing me to Christ, which has made all the difference.

Table of Contents

Introduction

There is a major problem in the real estate industry that is disrupting the careers of many agents. Real Estate agents are plagued by doubt of the alignment of their brokerage – the most important partnership of their career. Turnover is at an all-time high.

According to the National Association of Realtors (NAR), thirty-percent of agents say they have been with their firm for a year or less. In the first five years in the industry, 90-percent of agents fail. That means that ten-percent of agents are making the majority of sales and earning most of the commissions. These successful agents are the ones that make the industry so attractive. They are turning deal-after-deal, making lots of money as their own boss and raising their family on a flexible schedule. They're living the ultimate agent lifestyle.

So, what is the difference between the failing 90-percent and the successful 10-percent of agents? Broker alignment is one of the main reason. The foundation of the agent's business is the brokerage they choose to hang their license with. The brokerage partner impacts their marketing strategy, lead opportunities, work-life culture, level of support and commission splits. When an agent is not aligned with their brokerage, they instinctively doubt their business, pull back from marketing and prospecting, and start looking for greener grass. The agents that are fully aligned are able to go all-in for the long-haul, worry-free and focused on building their clientele and their team which results in high commission earnings and eventually the ultimate agent lifestyle.

The drastic difference in success rates can't be blamed on the agent. It's not the brokerage's fault either. It's the seductive cycle of desperation. Because of the high turnover rate, brokerages have responded by increasing their number of agents knowing that most won't be back next year. The Association of Real Estate License Law Officials (ARELLO) estimates that there are about 2 million active real estate licensees in the United States. There's a dog-fight going on over any breathing body with a license because the more added this year, the more chances of a few hundred dollars rolling in. It has become a competition of commission-splits that have become the smoke and mirrors that distract from the true elements of business building that the successful agents are wisely seeking.

The only way to create long-term success is to seek true alignment between the brokerage and the agent from the very beginning. And there is so much more to alignment than commission splits. This book presents a list of traits shared among the most successful agents that are worth your consideration when interviewing your potential brokerage. When you know what it takes to be a successful agent, you won't be distracted by the 'commission splits' conversation. Instead, you'll be equipped with the specific questions to ask your broker during your interview to find the perfect brokerage for you.

While interviewing hundreds of agents interested in joining my brokerage, Realty National, I quickly realized how unprepared the agents are when they are making the biggest decision in their career.

They expect for the person that is there representing the brokerage to just talk the whole time and sell them on their business model without regard to the agent's true needs or career trajectory. The agents hardly ever ask any questions to really understand what our company is about, what our core values are and what our company culture is like. Agents have become so used to this interaction that they are surprised when I ask them to explain their own business and life goals and how they want to grow over the next several years.

It's pretty crazy if you ask me. The broker owner is the one that is taking on all the liability when they bring on an agent and the agent is entrusting their business to the brokerage. For both parties to be successful, both must be aligned and feel really good about their decision. They need to take the time to get to know each other and see if it's a true fit for long-term success.

When things truly feel like a fit, an agent can focus on building a business rather than the doubt of their partnership. They can start building their brand within the company that they are with and invest money into marketing. They can connect with other agents in the office to create long-lasting friendships, find mentors, and build their team. They can rely on their team and the management to support them through the challenges. They can actually build the solid foundation that is required in order to create the ultimate agent lifestyle.

I've personally seen agents go from flat to flourishing when they find the right "home," as we call it. The most successful agents are able to leverage their brokerage to build a team around them who align with their greater vision for business and for life. I promise you that if you take this first step seriously, you will find the perfect brokerage for you. You'll be dedicated to staying with them long-term and you'll watch your business grow in a direction that you dreamed about while creating the ultimate agent lifestyle – the way you define it.

Instead, unfortunately most agents are easily swayed into making a decision that is not aligned with their goals and what's actually important to them. Many agents commit quickly to the first company that they meet, basing their choice strictly on commission splits. Then, when it doesn't work out, they blame the brokerage. My mission is to empower you to select a brokerage that is congruent with your own personal and business values from the beginning so you will actually achieve your ultimate lifestyle dreams.

Be the agent that puts your values and goals at the top of the agenda. Then interview several companies with the questions in this book and search for the truth of the brokerages you interview. You'll be able to sort through the clutter and find a fit much faster than you think. You'll make an educated decision to choose the perfect brokerage for you.

As you read, you'll first identify the common traits among successful agents and how you can seek to embody those traits. Then, I'll break down each question to ask during your interview and unveil how to dig for the gold in each one. To accompany this book, I've created for you the Agent Interview Guide.

It's a list of all of the questions, which you can print and take with you to your next interview to ensure you're asking the questions that keep YOUR values and goals at the top of the agenda. Get the Agent Interview Guide at: www.AgentLifestyle.com

Part 1

The Top 5 Traits of Successful Agents

In most states, it's very easy to get your real estate license and that definitely plays into the over saturation of agents. With about 2 million active real estate licensees in the United States, it's not easy to stand out from all the noise. Only 10% will succeed and the other 90% will be long gone within the first two years of business. If you can make it to $100,000 per year in this business, you are more than doubling the 2015 realtor national median gross income of $39,500 according to NAR.

You must know what separates successful agents from the rest so you can be among the top 10%. I have found that there a few characteristics that mega agents possess and will share them with you in this section.

1. Successful agents know their core values

"Your core values are the deeply held beliefs that authentically describe your soul" ~ John. C. Maxwell

Ever since I became involved in personal development in 2011, I could not imagine living without core values in business and in my personal life. I've used my core values to select my business partners, choose where to live, and meet my wife! Successful agents not only know their core values, they live by them as a road map for life.

Knowing your values will give you a solid foundation in your life and business and help guide all types of decisions from small daily ones to life-changing decisions. It also shows that you have standards of excellence in your behavior and for how others will treat you.

You don't need to make this complicated and you should be able to come up with solid core values under an hour. First, simply think of all the adjectives that describe you and your beliefs. Write them all down on a blank piece of paper and just keep brain dumping until you run out of things to write. Then, review it all and circle your top 10 that stand out the most to you and are your non-negotiables as I like to call them. This is where it gets tougher, I need you to select the top 5 and if you can't compromise between them and you like all 10, what you can do is create short statements or punch lines underneath the top five that would incorporate the other five words. And here you go, you have just created your core values or a set of beliefs that you will honor and live by.

2. Successful agents treat their business seriously

"Successful people are simply those with successful habits." ~ Brian Tracy

Real estate may be a flexible industry, but in order to succeed, you need to first see yourself as a true business owner and enter it with the willingness to treat this business seriously.

One of the hardest things to do is begin a real estate career part-time. Your potential clients want to see houses, they want to talk to their agent and they need information quickly. If the only time you have for your buyer is after 5pm and on weekends, they will become frustrated quickly and they will have a tough time finding a house especially, in a seller's market. As a part-time agent, it will be tough to find time to market yourself, hold open houses, make calls and do the other activities that bring your business.

Too many agents get into this business thinking they'll make thousands in commissions by helping their family members and friends. They fail to realize that even those people want a true professional with experience and systems to do the best job for them. If you're just getting started, then sorry to break this news to you, but you may not be their first choice. However, the good news is that all top producing agents started without any experience at all.

When you ask yourself about your level of seriousness, I want you to think about the hours that you are willing and able to commit to this business.

Just like any other business, you'll have to market your services by getting to know people in circles you aren't already familiar with. You may spend 20-30 hours per week on marketing and networking. You'll have to have a great contact management system for all the potential clients you'll be meeting. You'll spend another 20-30 hours reviewing contracts, negotiating, going to inspections and appraisals, and most importantly, database management. Time blocking will become a necessity in order to tackle all the daily tasks, track your performance by keeping statistics and find time to actually also work on the business and not just in it. This is where most agents fail, they tend to be very transactional and they don't take the time to work on their business to build a solid foundation that they can reap benefits from for years to come.

In order to assist your clients the right way, you need to learn how to write and review contracts, counters and addendums. You'll need excellent skills in negotiating and the ability to actually take a client through the whole buying or selling experience all the way through closing. As you might imagine, real estate school doesn't actually teach you the practical stuff that you would need so you have to commit to spending time educating yourself, learning from shadowing others, and learning through pure action taking. You'll have to be ready to dig for answers you don't already know and be okay with using your mistakes as lessons along the way.

Eventually, you'll get to the point in your business where you'll be able to control your own time and have more flexibility and freedom by leveraging your team, but that doesn't happen overnight.

This business requires you to work weekends, including Sundays. Especially as a new agent, you need to know you're most likely going to be working with buyers first and foremost because it is the easiest way to break into the business. In order to meet people in need of your assistance, you want to be doing open houses, which can consume large chunks of your weekend.

Whether it be a Saturday morning open house, which could last from 9 a.m. to 12 p.m. or maybe a Friday afternoon one from 4 p.m. to 7 p.m., these opportunities to receive recognition as a realtor require persistence and time. The open houses are held with the intent of expanding your client base and setting up appointments and showings throughout the week.

Most clients only have weekends available to view properties. Obviously this requires a massive amount of consideration when entering the field. Just like any business, you have to be willing to meet your clients where and when they need you to. If you don't, someone else will.

So, what will sacrificing weekends for business mean to you? Will you be able to cope with missing functions with family and friends for the sake of work or are those activities a staple in your life that you cannot remove? That Saturday soccer game for your son or daughter, or every Sunday morning at your local church? You may have to get creative to consider doing certain activities during the week where your schedule will have more flexibility.

Now, as your business grows, you start receiving more traffic and interest from clients, especially those that are referred to you by former clients, friends, and family. Luckily as your client base expands, your business can expand to the point where you can actually hire a couple buyer's agents. They can become the agents holding open houses or showing the properties to your clients on the weeknights and weekends. The perks of hard work and growth can finally pay off and provide the freedom you desire as you focus more of your energy representing sellers and listing their homes for sale.

To keep your eyes on the prize, you may want to choose a brokerage that challenges you to succeed in a fun and supportive way. For example, in our brokerage, we challenge every brand new agent to complete 3 transactions in their first 8 months, which we feel is reasonable under the right guidance and support. The challenge isn't just for the agent. We are all willing to step in to help out and answer questions as quickly as possible to help them succeed. After they reach their first goal, we want each agent to be closing a minimum of 10-12 transactions per year with our support and mentorship. If an agent can close 10-12 transactions per year in San Diego, they are more than likely earning a 6-figure income, which again, is more than double what an average realtor makes a year.

3. Successful agents seek support and guidance

"Surround yourself with only people who are going to lift you higher" ~ Oprah Winfrey

Mentors have always played a big role in the success of an agent. I find that agents that look for guidance and ask a lot of questions are the ones that grow the most and make the most progress. With the right mentor, their advice can save you a tremendous amount of time, which is our most valuable asset that we have; why re-invent the wheel when others' mistakes or successes will allow you to save time and energy in your development as an agent. You want to learn from other people's mistakes and watch your business flourish.

There could be several ways that support and guidance are provided in the real estate industry. Many times, there is a broker manager that is responsible for assisting all agents when they have transactional problems. This same manager could also be involved in training the agents on various real estate topics from entry level topics to more advanced.

Another popular model is agent-to-agent mentoring. This is where the seasoned agents are actually mentoring the brand new agents and they are getting compensated for doing so. In essence, this is a great set up since the brand new agents can sometimes relate better to the seasoned agents than they would to a manager that potentially is not even out there doing any transactions at all so his or her experience becomes limited after a while.

Another benefit of this set up is that the seasoned agents often times end up giving lead opportunities to the brand new agents that they don't have time to follow up with, which can later even lead to the brand new agent joining their team full-time if they show a level of desired performance and good conversion.

When you first get your real estate license, you need to be eager to learn and absorb every ounce of information. Outside of your brokerage's assistance in pointing you in the right direction, either internally or externally for specific trainings, you need to be proactive yourself. A great place to start when you are licensed is to ask your local real estate board to see what they offer at their place of business. You would be surprised how valuable they are to real estate agents and the education that they might be providing either at a very low cost or even free. They might offer a variation of trainings from in-person to webinars.

For example, you'll have to master the use of the MLS, multiple listing service. Your local MLS should have in-person or online classes so make sure to dive into those trainings right away so you can quickly find out the power of the MLS.

If you realize that great guidance and support will allow you to excel much faster, then you must look for a company that actually offers a business model that will assist you in your growth and help you achieve your specific business and lifestyle goals.

4. Successful agents are organized

"A place for everything and everything in its place"~
Benjamin Franklin

Organization is key when your business relies on clients. It's vital to keep their contact information, dates, and names organized. As you go out and hit the streets, this will be one of your first challenges. You'll never keep a bunch of business cards and your post-it notes and scribbled pieces of paper won't cut it as a professional high-producing agent.

Successful agents start with good habits and implement a CRM (contact relationship management) software of some sort from day one. Don't get hung up on what to use, an excel spreadsheet is better than not having anything, however, as you grow your database, transition into something more scalable.

Bottom line, the best CRM for you is the one that you will actually use, they all have pros and cons, so just pick one, study it and use it. Treat your database as the engine of your business. If you maintain communication with your database, your business will become easier and easier over time. You will no longer chase clients, new and existing clients will find you.

5. Successful agents delegate and outsource

"It is not that we have too little time to do all the things we need to do, it is that we feel the need to do too many things in the time we have." ~ Gary Keller

The concept of outsourcing is vital to the success of any business. If you allow your entire business to ride on your full control and execution, you will more than likely fizzle out or fail completely. A lack of trust in others not only reflects poorly on you, but turns people off to the idea of doing business with you.

When you outsource certain elements of your business that you aren't good at, you allow yourself to hire someone that is excellent at that task and improves your overall value. Plus, when you use professionals that can provide higher quality products and service than you could, it gives you the opportunity to excel in every other aspect of your business.

The first thing that agents need to outsource is transaction coordinating. Transaction Coordinating companies, or TC's, are worth every penny. These individuals or companies assist the agent and broker in the processing of a real estate file once you have an executed contract between a buyer and seller. Outsourcing this part of the transaction allows agents to fully focus on vital aspects of their operation such being there for their clients during the inspection, appraisal and final walk through to name a few. Agents should not be pushing paper on each transaction, but they should be always prospecting for new business by going to networking events, holding open houses and going to client appointments. Instead of attempting to save a dollar, outsource the transaction to a professional that will not only be able to produce a better experience for all parties involved, but will reduce your already overloaded responsibilities.

The second key task I would outsource is the marketing for the properties that you are selling. As your housing portfolio increases, the challenge of effectively marketing each property will grow larger than you can keep up with. This won't even be an issue until you obviously get your first listing, however, do yourself a favor and pay someone to do this for you. I realized early on when I was selling multiple houses per month that I can't stay on top of all the marketing and provide a superior service to my clients. I feel like most agents stop marketing when the market is hot or as we call it in the industry, a seller's market. In my opinion, they are missing on a huge opportunity to tell the public and the agent community that they are selling a home in a given neighborhood. This should be your priority when you have a house that you are selling even if you know that you will get an offer in the first few days. It's your chance to leverage that listing to the fullest extent to brand yourself, gather more business opportunities and have it out there on the internet and print for the long-haul, which further solidifies your experience.

Successful agents believe in delegation and outsource these tasks first and foremost as they focus their time on prospecting, developing systems for their business and growing a team, which will lead them to actually living the ultimate agent lifestyle that they so desire.

Part 2:

Ask The Right Questions

The following questions were specifically designed to help you start understanding each brokerage's identity as you go out there on your search for the perfect brokerage for you. The Agent Interview Guide I've made for you will facilitate your interview and allow you to easily compare and contrast the business models that exist in the real estate industry. As you read the questions, you will learn about the core reason for each one and what you might expect in certain scenarios. I truly believe that a brokerage that you fully align with is the first step to creating the ultimate agent lifestyle for yourself, so I want you to take this seriously from the moment you walk into each office that you are considering.

You can download the Agent Interview Guide to print and take with you to your interview at:
www.AgentLifestyle.com

1. What are the company's core values?

"Values are like fingerprints. Nobody's are the same, but you leave them all over everything you do."~ Elvis Presley

Every office should have core values that they fully believe in and live by. It's even better if these core values are personally selected by the agents themselves and evident in the company's brand. Our company used this democratic process to truly solidify who we are as an organization and develop accountability between all members. Now, we look to our core values in everything and use them as an anchor in our decisions, to review in our meetings, and in conversations with each other and our clients. It's powerful to have the whole team agree to and live by a set of common beliefs.

See if the company that you are considering has core values that resonate with you. If they don't, move on. Don't be distracted with perks like leads or a high split. Don't sacrifice your values for theirs. Core values determine the culture of the company and determine your long term happiness and success there.

2. What defines the brokerage? What is it known for?

"In a crowded marketplace, fitting in is a failure. In a busy marketplace, not standing out is the same as being invisible." ~ Seth Godin

Immediately after learning about the company's core values, you need to focus on what makes this brokerage stand out from its competitors. Even if this company does not have the opportunity to drastically differentiate themselves from the competition, you still need to see what the brokerage is known for and what their niche is.

Though a company's specialty may not limit the business it produces, you must know if this brokerage's specialty allows you to excel, and places you in the market that you desire.

For example, some companies may be known for selling luxury properties while others may be known for selling only coastal properties. Investigate for yourself. A quick review of a company's website should reveal their specialty as a business. If this specialty truly defines the brokerage, it should be evident on their website and should not require searching.

My brokerage specializes in working with investors, especially those who renovate single-family homes, and though it's not the only aspect of our business, our specialization in this is evident on our website. As a brokerage finds its niche, it tends to attract those agents that are attracted by their story and agents that can relate to them in some capacity. With a clearly stated identity and goal through our website and marketing, we are able to continue to attract agents that share a common goal as us. Once you select a brokerage where you truly connect with their story and identity, then, it's a pleasant experience as you feel that everyone speaks your language

That, in my opinion, is the ultimate place to land: somewhere where the goals of the brokerage and your professional goals are aligned.

Our agents know that when they join our company; they will hear investor language everywhere, they will see actual properties transformed from trash to treasure, and they will be offered opportunities to sell truly pristine homes. They will have access to off-market inventory since there is always a good amount of properties under construction and not yet listed on the market. They will be able to attend team building and educational events at actual construction sites.

They will be able to get into re-developing themselves if they find that of interest.

When your brokerage has a unique niche, it is easier for you to stand out amongst the thousands of agents out there because you have something unique to offer your clients. In our case, one example is our off-market properties and we train our agents to leverage this in the marketplace for their success.

Find a company that actually matches your vision! You don't have to fit a square puzzle piece in your circle of a vision. Search for a brokerage with the niche you desire and take advantage of their resources and brand recognition. Your brokerage should give you an advantage in the marketplace, not just be a placeholder.

3. Do you have anything I can leverage that is exclusive to your company that no other brokerage in the area has?

"You have to be unique and different and shine in your own way."~ Lady Gaga

It would be good for you to know if there is anything exclusive that the office that you are looking into has that others in the area don't. For example, there are brokerages that have an exclusive relationship with a relocation company, which could provide a stream of business to the agents that work for the company. Another example would be a brokerage's relationship with an asset management company for who they sell bank-owned properties, which, in turn, could lead to opportunities for the agents working at that brokerage.

Our brokerage, which works with many investors, has a unique opportunity that gives our agents a little edge on the market as they could leverage the off-market properties to set up future appointments for homes that haven't yet gone on the market but could be the perfect house for their client. The same off market properties are renovated and fully staged before being released which gives our agents access to beautiful properties that they can hold open houses at. This type of strategic relationship with a coinciding company could be a massive contribution to your potential business growth.

There are many ways that a brokerage can differentiate itself from others in your region. The important factor here is to know that any unique positioning can become a major asset to you as an agent with any brokerage but only if you're able to leverage it properly.

4. Do agents support and share trade secrets with one another?

"Power is gained by sharing knowledge, not hoarding it" ~ unknown

Is this company going to provide internal competition or will the company culture support you and other realtors within the brokerage?

It's really awful to hear of brokerages where agents don't share successes with one another. There are plenty of them out there. At these brokerages, agents view each other as competition and keep everything they're learning to themselves. This type of behavior usually develops in environments where resources are scarce. When agents have to go through a lot of blood, sweat and tears to learn a simple thing "the hard way", they feel like they'd give others an unfair advantage by sharing. They are operating from a fear mindset.

Environments that share openly are ones where resources are plentiful and the agents operate from a growth mindset.

Trading personal specialties, such as direct mail or follow up campaigns, can skyrocket your business in much shorter of a time frame than normal. Plus, the more willing you are to share, the more willing someone will be to share with you. This is why successful agents attend 'masterminds' to share information and grow their businesses. It's a win-win!

A healthy brokerage will have an atmosphere of encouraging and lifting up the whole. You've heard that a rising tide lifts all ships. That's how healthy businesses grow stronger.

Personally, in every company of mine, past and present, I have always set the stage for sharing between all of the partners, staff and co-workers. We have systems in place to encourage sharing ideas during team meetings, monthly masterminds, team building events and mentorship relationships. The energy makes our family of employees and agents stronger and allows us to actually enjoy the time we spend together.

Your goal should be to surround yourself with co-workers and people who hold an abundance mentality rather than a scarcity mentality. Build your own environment where an abundance of knowledge is encouraged, which will ultimately grow your wealth.

5. Is there support staff in place to help me when needed?

"Encourage, lift and strengthen one another. For the positive energy spread to one will be felt by us all" ~ *Deborah Day*

I find lack of support to be the biggest reason why most agents decide to leave brokerages, especially within the first 2 years of their career. As an agent, you need support regularly. Every transaction is unique and provides unique circumstances, which I like to refer to as an opportunity to grow. If you approach each challenge as a growth opportunity, you'll need to look to someone to teach you what you need to make the growth happen.

It's easy to get caught up in the emotion of a transaction, especially when it takes a turn for the worst. As one of my mentors says, "When emotions are high, intelligence is low." When things are going south, you need to talk to a third-party so you can have someone totally neutral to the transaction give you solid and sincere advice.

Support at a company will determine if you actually keep your deals alive all the way to closing. I hear of too many agents losing deals because emotions take over to the point where they get in a fight with the agent on the other side of the transaction. Any deal revolving around an argument will only lead to egotistical decisions not intended to give the best scenario for the clients.

The manager of my brokerage is excellent at being available and having a solution to every problem. We call him the "Fire Man" because he puts out fires for our agents day in and day out. He is the go-to guy that our agents call to help save their deal and he's darn good at it! He's extremely valuable to the individual agent and to the brokerage. He helps the agents grow through a finished deal rather than learn through a lost one or never at all.

Getting support when you need it most will allow reason to trump any actions that will only harm the deal further. With all that said, please make sure that the company that you are considering has an experienced staff person readily available to handle your urgent issues.

6. Will the support staff go to a client appointment with me?

"A true friend supports you because they want to see you succeed" ~ Ms Moem

Beginning your career, you will more than likely not be as polished as a seasoned agent and therefore will stumble through appointments. Unfortunately, any hint of unpolished service will be viewed as unprofessional in comparison to some of the agents that the client might be interviewing. Though this is expected, the option to call in support from experienced veterans on your staff will exponentially enhance your ability to represent the seller or buyer and train you in the process.

The support staff may attend an appointment with you or welcome you and your client to meet with them in the office. These veterans will be able to provide valuable insight for every situation especially those that you would never expect as a new agent. They will be able to handle different objections that the client might have if you don't have the answers you need about the process or their unique situation.

Watching the improved interactions between our agents and their clients in the office when our manager sits in those meetings emphasizes the importance of wisdom for an agent. Not only does the agent walk away with an increased education, but they are forced into the conversation as a partner, not an employee, which purely helps the client that much more.

With this type of support, your nerves will definitely go down and confidence will go up so if this is something that you absolutely need, consider finding a brokerage that offers this service.

7. Do you have a self-study training website for the agents?

"Knowledge will bring you the opportunity to make a difference." ~ Claire Fagin

Most companies provide agents with some form of general training. The most common is for the brokerage to prepare their own in-house trainings to educate the agents on the industry, the brokerage, and the expectations as an agent within that brokerage. These videos and articles are usually housed on a website available only for agents with a unique login.

This concept of company education helps ensure that agents within the brokerage align with the approach of the company.

Other companies have partnered with a 3rd party training company that has prepared general training videos for agents that aren't necessarily linked to the specific brokerage. These are usually available online or could include in person workshops and trainings.

Some companies provide advanced courses that require an investment from the agent.

Once you understand what exactly is involved in training and on-boarding as a new agent in a potential brokerage, you have to decide what is most important to you.

More isn't necessarily better. You don't need a zillion trainings; you only need the training that applies to you in the moment you need it. At times, rather than a step by step guided approach, many agents are given a library of content that leaves them unsure which step to take. The simpler the approach, the better the chance that the education is followed and utilized by agents within the brokerage.

8. Are the agents in the office open to me shadowing them?

"A leader is one who knows the way, goes the way, and shows the way." ~ John C, Maxwell

I usually tell our newer agents to go in and talk to the other seasoned agents and see if they could follow one of them for a few open houses. I encourage them to shadow as many agents as possible in order to pick up different methods that fit best to their personality. Shadowing an experienced agent at an open house allows you to pick up hints on client interaction and company display of houses. This alone could speed up your training and boost your confidence with open houses on your own.

This is not an opportunity that is available in every brokerage. If you are a newer agent or one looking to level-up your current business, I would highly suggest seeking out a company where agents offer this support. The benefits are unbelievable and the growth comes quicker than you could ever get on your own.

Becoming a part of a successful office/team where you surround yourself with successful people will flood you with wisdom and prepare you to prosper as an agent.

9. Do you allow part-time agents to be part of the company?

"Hard work doesn't guarantee success, but improves its chances" ~ B.J. Gupta

There are many different approaches to brokerages in the real estate world. Some models are very friendly towards part-time agents and some models don't want any part-time agents at all.

Starting as a part-time agent is a rather common way to enter the real estate industry. The addition of part-time agents is generally not a negative idea, however it can come with consequences as brokerages can become filled with a distant and lackluster staff if too many of the agents are part-time.

What you will find a lot in the industry is that many new agents actually have full-time jobs as they try to break into this business as a realtor. At our brokerage, we allow a few part-time agents on a case by case basis, but we title them *transitional agents*, as we help them transition into full-time agent roles within their first year.

Many brokerages actually make it their goal to get as many agents as possible to join their company, whether full or part-time, because they want to hold the largest possibility of a transaction closing. Though this can be effective for the brokerage and it will make them look large in numbers, it is not always effective for the new or part-time agent as you could get lost in the mix and might have a difficult time finding role models and mentors to seek support from.

Make sure you position yourself in a company that can support you at every level and really aligns with what you need in the immediate future and beyond.

10. Do you allow teams to work at your brokerage?

"Unity is strength, when there is teamwork and collaboration, wonderful things can be achieved" ~ Mattie J.T. Stepnak

As a new agent, it may be hard for you to envision a full team, but to truly maintain a lifestyle of flexibility and ease, having a team is the only way to do it. Down the road, you might find yourself wanting to be part of a team or manage a team underneath you. I've seen husband-and-wife teams, family teams with parents and their children, even a group of agents that work well together and decide to join forces as a team to build the business faster.

Some agents start their agent career right from the beginning by working on a team. This is a great way to break into the business, gain experience, and quickly overcome your biggest fear of being new. When you join a team, most of the time what will happen is that all of the business is going to go under the main team leader. So what takes place in most team structures is that the team leader will give you some leads of potential clients to work with. Then, when you do actually close on the transaction with those leads, it is not your name as the agent on the contract, it's actually the team leader's name on everything and he or she takes the credit for the production.

You will get compensated for your efforts, however the commission split will be negotiated and determined between you and the team leader, not the owner of the brokerage. The team leader negotiates and determines the split with the owner first and foremost before he or she joined the brokerage. So if you decide to join his or her team, you are technically working under the team leader, however your license hangs under the owner.

I find that a good amount of agents start this way and as you get more and more experience, you might choose to branch out on your own or maybe even start a team yourself. Some choose to just stay with the team leader because he or she keeps feeding you business, which means you don't have to worry about farming, marketing and doing all the things that a full-time professional agent should be doing.

Another way that you might be able to partner up with another agent is just working on certain leads together, but not the entire book of business that you might have in your pipeline. This is something that will allow you a little bit more flexibility because, in this scenario, you are not committed to doing all of your business with that agent. It's also a great way to see who you work well with as you get to know each other better on a per-transaction basis. Remember, each transaction has its ups and downs and what better way to learn about each other but in real life scenarios. This set up also allows you to have these types of arrangements with more than just one agent because you are not tied to anyone fully like you are under the team leader structure.

For example, if you are working with a particular client in an area that you don't do much business with, you could work with another agent that does and give that agent a percentage of the commission and everyone wins while you provide a superior service to your client.

There are many ways to set up teams, so explore all of your options before going that route. I am a big fan of teams as I strongly believe that everyone has different strengths and weaknesses so instead of spending all your time improving your weakness, find an agent that actually flourishes in the area that you don't. You will find that your collective efforts will produce more success when everyone operates the majority of their time in their strength zone.

You might also find that some offices don't allow teams at all. Be mindful of that because if you ever decide that you would like to partner with someone in the future, then you might have to switch to a different brokerage that will actually allow you to form a team. Switching brokerages has a massive impact on your current and future business. The disruption typically costs agents 20 percent of their sales volume in the first year following the switch.

Bottom line, teams allow you to have more freedom, flexibility and success on the journey to the ultimate agent lifestyle and that's why at our company, we choose to spend quite a bit of time helping our agents formulate teams since there are so many ways of structuring them. We make sure that it's fair to both sides and that the agents clearly write out each other's expectations that cover the responsibilities and compensation.

11. What should I expect at the team meetings?

"If everyone is moving forward together, then success takes care of itself." ~ Henry Ford

I highly encourage you to ask the owner if you can attend an office meeting before you make your final decision. You will learn a ton about the company, the agents at the company and the culture just from this one meeting alone.

In the real estate industry, team meetings are generally not well attended. Asking about the attendance demographic of the team meetings can give you a lot of insight to what level of value they may bring to you.

As an incoming agent, meetings could be an incredible opportunity for you to create connections with other agents within your office. However, just because a brokerage has a large amount of agents, does not mean that the attendance at those meetings will be through the roof. You will be very surprised to find that the percentage of the agents that actually come to the office meetings is much slimmer than expected. A majority of large brokerages that I have seen hold around a 25-30% attendance at their meetings.

A lack of attendance at team meetings will reflect the culture of a company pretty effectively. Though there are many possible reasons for this, a majority of the time, it boils down to agents not receiving enough value from a meeting to make the commitment worth their time.

Find out whether or not these meetings will be internally or externally ran and how the information will be presented to the agents. Many companies outsource their meetings to outside vendors such as escrow officers, title reps, or lenders to train on their niche. Though this can be effective, you have to be aware of whether or not those vendors are merely pushing their services onto the brokerage or are legitimately teaching for the benefit of the agents.

If a company can provide important information or training consistently, it would become clear to agents that they would miss vital information if they don't attend, so they may have higher attendance rates because of the value provided.

Brokerages with smaller agent count such as ours, generally see a higher percentage of attendance due to the family culture and the value that is intentionally provided to each agent. If team meetings are important to you, you'll want to work with a company that can effectively use the time that they have specifically set out to meet and grow as a unit.

12. Do you do any team building events together as a company?

"If you're not having fun, you're doing it wrong" ~ Alex Bogusky

Team events are a great way for the agents to connect on a personal level and enjoy one another's company. When you have the opportunity to get to know your co-workers on a deeper level, it sparks opportunities to grow your business and support theirs.

These events can vary from the typical happy hour at a local bar to an afternoon of bowling. The biggest challenge is organizing them so if there is no one actually in charge of putting them on the calendar, notifying and engaging the agents, then, the chances are that they will never actually take place.

At my brokerage, we stay consistent by doing some sort of a team event every other month. It's our Operations and Marketing Director's responsibility to ask our agents for suggestions at our team meetings, then actually select one and put it into play for the upcoming month. They are not mandatory, but because they are fun and peer voted, they end up being well attended.

13. Does the company promote sharing goals with each other?

"A goal is a dream with a deadline" ~ Napoleon Hill

There is something powerful about writing goals down. Simply tracking your future steps with logged checkpoints simplifies success and makes goals attainable rather than up in the air.

It's great to think about your goals and to write them out for yourself. But research shows that sharing your goals out loud with someone else drastically improves the probability of achieving them. Sharing your goals with other agents in your industry will allow you to feel instant accountability and also encourages others to help you achieve your goal by providing insights and resources.

As you share goals, you are then held responsible for the effort towards and eventual completion of those tasks. Your conviction to backup your speech will assist your success and completion of your goals. Additionally, you gain the camaraderie with your co-workers that only comes with a team-oriented accomplishment. Having an openness about the struggle that comes along with striving for a goal allows individuals within a company to come together as a family and support one another.

14. Does your company support any charitable organizations?

"We make a living by what we get, but we make a life by what we give." ~ Winston Churchill

Many companies either support one main organization or spread their support out to multiple organizations without direct commitment to one. Association with a non-profit can help build positive company culture and can create a common cause for the agents to support. Look for a company with an option for agents to contribute because it will allow honest support and choice and give the agents ownership over the giving. This camaraderie also provides agents with time to connect with each other and build upon relationships as they are serving and volunteering together.

Our brokerage provides agents with the option of giving $50 per transaction into an account that is specifically designed for different charity events and donations. Over the years, we've been able to accumulate several thousand dollars into this account and we vote at our team meetings which organizations we will support with the donations. Though this may not be the only way a company can become involved, it would be good to know if there is a cause you can get behind while you join a brokerage.

15. Does your company offer lead opportunities?

"Nothing of value comes without being earned" ~ Michael Jordan

Many brokerages offer an array of leads to their agents. Because true leads can result in sales and eventual commissions for agents, this is clearly an important trait to consider when choosing a brokerage. Some brokerages offer leads to only a select few agents that meet certain requirements and are willing to follow certain processes and standards in order to receive them. This type of structure will have a CRM tied to it that will allow for tracking and follow up. These agents will usually have a team lead that they meet with weekly in order to review their progress and practice objection handling and much more.

In my opinion, this is the best structure, as it creates accountability for everyone involved and with the right organization and systems, this will result in highest conversion rates of leads to actual clients. Expect to pay a referral fee to the owner in this type of setup as it takes a lot of resources to make this work efficiently and for it to be effective. The referral fee will vary from company to company.

Some brokerages just give out leads randomly in a round-robin type of format to every single agent that's in the company but they don't really track any of the leads and how the agents are converting them. It's basically just a value-add they say that they offer. However most of those leads are very hard to convert to begin with, because if you don't have accountability and structure behind it, the chances of converting these leads is very low. In this type of setup, the owner usually won't charge a referral fee and they will just let the agent basically work the leads and if they convert them, great, if not, they won't even know. I personally don't like this structure because I feel that the true opportunity behind these leads is being lost and it could potentially create a negative customer experience.

Simply getting leads handed to you will not be enough to convert them. The biggest thing that you will have to remember is that to be successful with leads of any type, you'll need a CRM and a follow-up system in place.

16. Are your agents able to represent themselves on personal transactions?

"Real estate cannot be lost or stolen, nor can it be carried away. Purchased with common sense, paid for in full, and managed with reasonable care, it is about the safest investment in the world." ~ Franklin D. Roosevelt

Eventually, as an agent you may have the desire to profit from the renovation and redevelopment of a property. If you foresee this desire, clarify before joining a brokerage if this transaction would be allowed so that you do not run into difficulties later down the line.

Because of our roots in investing, my brokerage allows our agents to get involved in redevelopment, as we are fully aware of the risk and liability and have proper disclosures and insurance in place to protect the agent and the owner.

Some companies have a rule in place where they pay you a different commission split on your own personal residence or they will ask you to involve another agent from the office so you're not representing yourself on your own purchase or sale.

Others hold policies that ban against this due to the liability that may fall on the owner of the brokerage. So be mindful of asking this question so you know what the potential is down the road.

Almost all rules against this are put in place to avoid potential risk and liability. It's not a reason to avoid a brokerage, but worth knowing in advance so you don't assume and get blindsided when you're ready to expand into this arena.

17. What type of commission schedule do you follow and what will be my split?

"Price is what you pay. Value is
what you get." ~ Warren Buffett

You must know what value the brokerage brings to the table before discussing commissions and fees. Once you are sure a brokerage is able to offer you what you need to grow your business and aligns with your core values, then it's time to talk money.

There are many different commission models that brokerages use so I will cover a couple of them and point out some key differences.

One of the oldest and most traditional models is a commission split that is based on your production. At the beginning of the year, you start at a base commission split and as your production in the given year goes up, your commission split goes up. However, it then resets at the end of the year to the base commission split with a calendar year reset.

There is an obvious downside to this model. Let's say, for example that you have a slow start to the year, which means your split won't increase much, but then, you kick it into a high gear towards the end and your commission split goes up because of it. You are only able to take advantage of the higher commission split for a couple months until the January 1st reset happens and you are back at your base.

The second model, you also have a commission split that is based on your production, except the difference is that you actually have a cap set as to what you will pay the company within an entire year. You start at a base commission split as well, but you might be able to eliminate your commission split to the company at some point during the year once you reach the cap that is set. You will then be able to keep 100% of the commission going forward till the reset on January 1st. I have seen commission split caps that the agent will pay to the company vary from about $15,000 to $40,000 and it's all based on where you are in the country.

Unfortunately, the same negative exists with this model, as you can only take advantage of the higher commission split for a couple months or so until the January 1st reset.

Then, there is the flat fee model, which basically has no commission split, because you pay a fee per transaction to the company and you keep 100% of your commission outside of the transaction fees and any other administrative, insurance and office fees. This is a model that does not bring in much profit to the company per transaction so it relies on a high volume of transactions which means they bring on a lot of agents. Due to this, there tends to be less agent support and not a well defined culture, but can be extremely effective for high producing agents with a complete grasp on the market and their brand. I have seen companies charge anywhere from $295 to $495 per transaction outside of the other fees that I mentioned.

The commission schedule that we chose to implement at Realty National upon opening was the rolling commission schedule. In this model, an agent starts with a commission split based on their production, and their split rises as their production goes up, however it never actually resets at the end of the calendar year like the other models that I covered earlier. Every time there is a closing, we look at the Gross Commission Income for the past year from the actual day of the closing, then, based on where that year's total of production falls on the commission schedule, that's the commission split that will be applied to calculate the agent's portion.

The reason we decided to go with this model is that no matter when an agent has a high production month, he or she will be able to use that high production for commission split calculations for a whole year, which will give him or her the ability to remain at a higher commission split. The negative, for some agents, is that this commission schedule comes with accountability, as you can just as easily regress in your commission split. This model is harder to keep track of for the owner, however, if applied correctly, it benefits the agent for their efforts and also has accountability to keep them on track so they don't regress, and only improve on their commission split.

You will hear of so many different variations of commission schedules in the industry so please get clarity on what each company offers that you interview. However, focus on the value that your perfect brokerage provides outside of just commission schedules. Don't compromise your values for a higher paycheck and remember that 100% of no commission is still no commission. Final word of caution: you usually get what you pay for.

18. Are there other fees outside of the commission split that the company charges?

"False expectations take away joy." ~ *Sandra Bullock*

Many fees exist outside of commission splits or flat fee payments, so you need to enter a brokerage with the knowledge of the financial commitments you'll be taking on.

There are many different things that a brokerage can charge the agent a fee for. The most common cost to the agent is Errors and Omissions Insurance. Errors and Omissions insurance, or EandO, is a costly, but necessary expense to the broker that covers the agent in case of any lawsuit that arises from a transaction where the agent in a broker's office was involved. You want to ask the broker about how they charge for the EandO Insurance, whether or not it is per transaction expense or a lump sum per year, and if that amount varies from year to year. Also, in case of potential lawsuits, you should affirm whether or not they provide any assistance in attorney costs.

Another common charge is a technology or administration fee. These amounts could vary and usually they are charged per month or per transaction. This usually will cover anything from websites to administrative assistance, all of which are designed to assist in the ease of work for agents.

At brokerages that are branches or franchises of a larger company, the agents are usually required to pay a franchise fee to carry the recognized name of the company. So if the company that you are interviewing is a franchise, there will most likely be a franchise percentage that you will have to pay on every single transaction. This percentage can vary anywhere from 1% to as high as 8% in certain companies. The typical amount is about 5% to 6% of the gross commission from each transaction that's being paid to the corporate office. Smaller companies usually will not carry such fees.

I encourage you to look for a company that is very transparent about their fee structure and the reasons behind them all so you don't have to dig to find out or learn about them once you already made the decision to join. That should be a sign of what's to come if you stay with such company, so you might consider finding another company sooner rather than later.

19. Is there a rewards program in place if I recommend another agent to join the company?

"Supporting another's success won't ever dampen yours." ~ Purple Tasche

The concept of a referral rewards program has become rather common. Generally, agents would receive some level of compensation for the production of the agent that they refer to the brokerage that ends up joining. Most of the time, the referring agent must be with the brokerage in order to receive this compensation. Word of mouth is the most powerful marketing that a company can have so companies tend to reward those that promote the company to others.

When meeting with a brokerage, discover the simplicity of calculating your actual reward with the company for either suggesting a new agent or gaining a reward for the incoming agent's closings on an ongoing basis. Look for as little ambiguity in this as possible; the more straightforward it is, the easier it is for you to get behind the concept and the company.

There a few companies which offer a profit sharing concept in which you are rewarded as long as you and the correlating agent remain with the company.

If the rewards payouts are based on the profitability of the company, then you actually have no control over that and you will never know what that actual reward will be until it's given to you. Remember, you will never have access to the accounting books of the company so it's always going to be a mystery.

I personally like to reward our agents for recommending our company to other agents. If we find that they are a fit for our company, we document who referred them and reward the referring agent each time that the agent he or she referred has a closing. It's very black and white so you actually know exactly what you will get and it goes on as long as both agents are with the company.

Bottom line, a rewards program of any kind is an ability for you to generate some passive income on the side for just simply sharing your excitement about the company that you are with to other colleagues in the real estate industry.

.

Part 3:

Licensed Investor Seeking a Brokerage

This section is for a real estate investor that is looking to get his or her real estate license or already has a license but has not found the perfect brokerage yet.

At Realty National, we deal with a lot of investors due to our strategic relationship with FortuneBuilders, a premier real estate education company. We always encourage our investors to have someone on their team that has a real estate license to allow them to run their business more efficiently. Often, our investors will ask me these two questions: Why should I get licensed? And once I do get licensed, how do I find an investor-friendly brokerage? These are both very valid questions and I will answer them here.

Why an Investor Should Have a Real Estate License

The first reason is to get access to the MLS, Multiple Listing Service. Once you have access to the local MLS, you can do your own research, learn the market quicker and be able to do a detailed comparative market analysis on your own. You will also be able to create property searches that will allow you to receive notifications the moment a property gets listed based on criteria that you are seeking. Getting a property under contract is all about speed. The quicker you can call the listing agent, the higher the chances of being able to get your offer submitted and accepted.

I always advise investors to ask for the listing agent to represent them. This incentivizes the listing agent as they are able to also be your buyer's agent and make both sides of the commission. As an investor, you are not after the commission, you want to acquire the property so you can rehab it and sell it for a profit. However, some agents will not want to represent both sides of the transactions, which is totally okay. You can represent yourself and keep the commission or credit back to the seller.

The second reason is being able to access properties on your own. As a licensed investor, you don't have to bother the listing agent or another agent to show you properties that might have potential. You can go on your own to visit potential properties and with a trained eye, you can make quick decisions. Again, it's all about speed.

If you can find out about an opportunity on the MLS, you could immediately call the listing agent to get some details and arrange to call them back within an hour. Then, you could go see the property to analyze the repairs and the after-repair value (ARV) on your own. You'll be able to call the listing agent back with an offer price and terms before you even leave the property. With this speed of decision-making, you'll have a higher probability of getting your offer in front of the seller.

The listing agent can then write up the contract and send it to you for signatures via email. You sign the offer electronically and there you go! Your offer is ready to be presented to the seller within an hour from the time you got the notification about the property. This is one of the biggest advantages over any other investor that is not licensed or doesn't have an agent on their team. Great investment opportunities sometimes only last a few hours or even minutes so you need to act quickly.

The third reason is the ability to connect with other real estate agents and build long-lasting business relationships. As a licensed investor, you can now attend agent events. Most cities have caravans, which are basically agent gatherings where agents share what properties they have for sale, get feedback from one another and go drive the properties based on a route organized by the caravan staff. In San Diego, you can literally be at a different caravan almost every day of the week. The average number of agents at a caravan is around 30, but I've seen them host up to 100 agents.

This is a great networking opportunity that you should absolutely take advantage of so you can get to know other fellow agents and they can get to know you. Some caravans have a spot where the agents that have buyers can share their buyer needs, this is where you can raise your hand and let them know that you are a licensed investor and that you are looking for ugly homes that need renovation and that you would like them to represent you if they have such opportunities.

By doing this, you just told every agent in the room that they can make money with you when they hear of such property. This will usually have several agents approach you after the meeting to discuss opportunities or your wish list. The trick to this, just like with anything else if you want to be successful at it, is to be consistent. You can't expect to go once in awhile and get business from the agents right away. You need to keep showing your face at these event and be consistent.

You want to focus on building relationships and this is the easiest way to be in front of many agents at once where they actually will listen. There are many other agent events that you can attend outside of caravans. Usually, each real estate board will have their own events that they put on for their members only. Then, there are the big agent events such as the annual National Association of Realtors events and state events as well. I can't stress enough how important face-to-face interaction is in this fast-paced business.

The last reason that I would like to bring up is the ability to make additional income. As an investor, you are most likely marketing to generate seller leads. These leads statistically prove to qualify for your cash purchase program only about 2 out of 10 times. The other 8 could be potential listing opportunities. The seller that you are meeting with will need to sell so why not try to find a way to help them based on their situation and connect them with a professional real estate agent? I never would recommend that a newly licensed investor take on the listing as they are not educated enough on this process and they would actually do a disservice to the seller.

I encourage licensed investors to refer these listing opportunities to another professional, full-time agent. When you take this server approach, you will be able to put yourself in the strongest probability to help the potential client, plus your agent can actually walk away with a listing agreement. Once this property sells, you could easily ask for a 25% referral fee back to you from the agent that you recommended to the seller. This is a pretty typical referral fee in the industry, however, it's all negotiable.

I am an advocate of you going to the appointment with an agent, and as you listen to the seller's situation, you can formulate your solution based on their actual needs, and not just your specific agenda. This will represent incredible customer service on your end and it will allow you to build trust much easier.

As a licensed investor, you can also refer all your calls on your For Sale signs to a full time professional agent and collect referral commissions when the agent that you referred closes on a house with a buyer. Not every buyer will fall in love with your house that you renovated, but they will buy something so why not have them work with your agent. This way, you all win.

Let me close with this, there are rumors out there that if you are a licensed investor, it puts you at a higher liability and it won't allow you to do certain things. I'm not an attorney, nor do I give legal advice, but I do believe that if you do the business with full ethics and integrity and you disclose the fact that you are a licensed real estate agent anytime you put a property under contract to buy or when you go to sell your own renovation, then, you have nothing to worry about.

I do suggest that you contact your state's real estate department and find out what you need to put on your marketing when you are a licensed agent and are sending out marketing directly to sellers. Again, it's all about disclosures and informing the public that you are a licensed agent doing business as a principal in your investing business. When in doubt, always lean on the side of over-disclosing, as you should have nothing to hide.

How to Find an Investor-Friendly Brokerage

When an owner of a brokerage hangs an agent's license, whether the agent is an investor or not, they take on the responsibility and liability for which they pay insurance yearly. If there is an issue that arises from a transaction or from an agent just doing everyday business, the broker needs to step in, take responsibility and resolve it with the agent involved.

Most brokerages don't have the additional EandO insurance that covers the activity of investors, so they do not allow their agents to be involved in personal investing and re-developing properties. This is one of the biggest challenges that most licensed investors run into when searching for an investor-friendly brokerage.

As a licensed investor, you have to showcase the value you bring the brokerage in order for them to consider taking on the additional EandO insurance cost and liability.

The best way to present the value that you can bring to any owner of a brokerage is to show them how you will be able to create business opportunity that leads to transactions closing, since that's usually the only way that he or she makes any revenue.

What I find that most investors do wrong when they go out to find an investor-friendly brokerage is that, out of the gate, they say; "I just got my license but I buy, fix and sell properties for a living. I am looking for a brokerage where I can just hang my license as I don't want to do any realtor stuff. I just need access to the MLS and access to properties." This approach does not sound attractive to any owner of a real estate brokerage. It's all about you and you are not providing any value to the owner. They will quickly disengage and not be thrilled to bring you on board.

Now, if you go into this same interview and you say something like this; "I am a licensed real estate investor, I buy, fix and sell properties for a living. Due to my business, part of my marketing strategy is to send out a lot of direct mail to potential sellers, however, statistically proven, only maybe 2 out of 10 of the potential sellers that I will meet with, can actually qualify for my cash purchase program. The other 8 will still likely need to sell, however, they might be better off putting the property on the open market. I was wondering if there is an agent in your office that you might be able to connect me with. I'd like to see if I can create some synergy with someone whom I can actually bring to these appointments so we can really provide the best solution for the potential client." Now, doesn't this sound much better?

This speaks massive value to the owner of the brokerage as you just offered to bring listing opportunities to their office. So, you got their attention and that's the first thing that you are after. Here is the kicker, as you continue your conversation; "Oh, remember those 2 opportunities that I might be able to buy to renovate, well, I will most likely have the same agent that goes to these appointments with me, sell these properties for me, as I am not interested in acting as an agent selling my own properties. I would much rather have a professional agent sell them for me as I know he or she would do a much better job and actually get me more money than what I can get on my own." With this statement, you basically just told the owner of the brokerage that they might have a shot on doing business on every single opportunity that comes your way from your marketing efforts. Now, isn't that wonderful?!

Trust me, you will have full attention of most owners of any brokerage at this point as they understand what it means to have repeat business come their way. This is where you don't guarantee anything, but just ask for introductions to a couple agents in his or her office to see if you will find a fit with one of them. You can mention that once you decide who you see yourself working with best, then, that's the office where you will most likely want to hang your license as it would only make sense to be under the same company.

Once you interview the agents that you are introduced to, then, you look back at all the questions that I suggested in part 2 and use them to find the perfect brokerage for you so you can make an educated decision based on all factors, not just commission splits.

I suggest that you look for a company that offers a lot of support where they can actually help you in market and deal analysis so that you can be more efficient and become an area expert much quicker. The quicker you become successful, the quicker the owner of the brokerage benefits from your mutual business relationship and the agent from their office that you selected will have more business come their way than they can handle.

Part 4:

Assess Your Current Situation

Whether you are looking to join your first brokerage or you are considering a switch, this part of the book is designed to assess your current situation. It will provide suggestions of the steps you could take to help you avoid making a hasty decision.

Get the Most from Your Current Brokerage

If you are actually doubting yourself if where you are currently is a right fit for you, then you might first want to look into it a bit deeper before you jump ship. I find that agents usually get into this headspace when their production drops. They tend to blame their current brokerage for their lack of success.

I suggest that you first analyze your own situation and see what has changed from when you were doing well to now. Are you able to find any major distractions, patterns or maybe lack of action in certain areas?

If that's the case, schedule a meeting with the owner or manager at your current brokerage to discuss those short falls and see if he or she will be willing to help you get back on track and keep you accountable. I find that agents sometimes are not proactive enough in taking advantage of what's available to them at their current brokerage. Remember, that most owners and managers want to see you succeed as it reflects back on them and the company that they are building.

Secondly, if certain things are not clear to you, then, use some of the questions in this book to get the clarity that you need in order to make you feel right about staying. Don't leave your current brokerage until you explore all they have to offer. You may find that there are training options and opportunities you didn't know about. Also, discuss your objections with your broker or leadership and see if there's something they are willing to do to help you succeed. At the end, you want to achieve a feeling of trust and total "buy in" so you can truly call the company that you are with your perfect brokerage. Once you do that, you can be well on your way to creating the ultimate agent lifestyle.

To assist you in this process, get the Agent Interview Guide at: www.AgentLifestyle.com

Switching Brokerages Without Burning Bridges

If you have done what I suggested above and you are still not fully satisfied with your current company, then, it might be time to consider other options. However, don't burn bridges behind you. The industry is small and word gets out quickly so whenever you decide to leave your current brokerage, do it with grace.

I personally think that you should be transparent with your current owner or leadership about your feelings and you might be surprised of what comes from it. He or she might actually be able to help you find a place that is a better fit for you.

Take your time and don't rush so you are not stuck in the same situation with a new brokerage later. Follow the suggestions in this book and come up with a clear understanding as to what you are looking for in your perfect brokerage. Know what your primary needs are and how your brokerage can meet (and exceed) those needs. Understand your strengths and weaknesses and find a brokerage that will compliment both.

Lastly, be honest with yourself and take stock in what your real estate business needs and then explore which brokerage can best serve those needs.

For Comparison: The Recruitment Process at Realty National

I wanted to share with you our process to shine some light on what you might expect out there in your search. Every owner has a different approach but here is ours that we have refined over the years. Keep in mind, that we are a selective brokerage so before we bring anyone on board, we want to make sure that it feels right for both parties.

First, a potential agent reaches out to us by finding us on social media, our website or an advertisement.

Second, we schedule their first interview with our manager, Bryan. Our goal in this meeting is to ask them questions that will further allow us to understand their character and core values. We have about 20 questions that we tap into so we can keep the conversation going and keep getting to know each other. This part usually takes about an hour. Bryan finishes the interview with a tour of our office and our parent companies that we are strategically aligned with. The agent receives our company informational packet to review at their leisure and see what other questions come to mind as they think about potential alignment.

It's important to note that at this first interview, we never discuss commission splits and our manager, Bryan, sets the expectations about this right at the start.

Next, Bryan and I meet to review all his notes and we have a discussion about each potential agent that we might be considering bringing on board to join the family. If we feel that the agent might be a good fit for our brokerage and vice versa, we schedule a second interview with Bryan and myself.

This 2nd interview allows me to assess the potential agent's strengths and the areas in which they will need the most support in order to be successful. We also cover our commission schedule and dive into the details of the support and services we offer that will be specifically beneficial to the individual agent or team.

This meeting usually takes an hour or even two hours if it's going great and we feel that we are aligning well. At the end, if we both feel good about each other, we extend an invitation for the potential agent to visit our team meeting to meet most of our agents and get a feel for our culture.

At the team meeting, we usually open with a game of corn hole and a mimosa. Whoever wins gets "Realty

National Bucks" that can be exchanged for services like Done-For-You-Marketing or company apparel to name a few. It's a pretty laid-back environment of mostly type-A drivers, so being a fit is important for not just the new agent but the seasoned agents that are already members of our team. I want the agent to determine if they can see themselves as part of our family and I also want to see how our current agents feel about the potential new family member.

This interviewing process is substantially more involved than what other brokerages have in place, however, I am a true believer that both parties need to take their time in making one of the most important decisions for them both. I want every agent that ends up joining our family to feel like they have found the perfect brokerage and I want to be proud of the fact that this agent will be representing our brand in our local community.

Our brokerage is not the perfect brokerage for everyone, but if you want to explore us to see if it could be a fit for you, please consider scheduling a meeting with our manager, Bryan. You can email us at opportunities@realtynational.com. We'd love to meet you! Don't forget to bring your questions!

Download the Agent Interview Guide at:
www.AgentLifestyle.com

About the Author

Randy Zimnoch rides to his office in a golf cart wearing a ball cap and flip flops. He is the owner of Realty National, a boutique real estate brokerage with several locations. Over the last 5 years, Randy has mentored his San Diego team of agents to sell $300,000,000 worth of real estate. He has trained thousands of real estate professionals from stages across the country including Boston, Chicago and Las Vegas. His ultimate lifestyle includes plenty of adventure. He's jumped out of planes, climbed Mt. Kilimanjaro, volunteered in Haiti and traveled to over 25 countries. After interviewing hundreds of agents, Randy understands the qualities that make an agent successful and able to live the ultimate lifestyle. For more information and to get the free Real Estate Agent Interview Guide, visit: www.agentlifestyle.com

94854186R00059

Made in the USA
Columbia, SC
01 May 2018